Copyright

Copyright © 2023 by Pastor Francis Elimimian

Publication data on file with National Library and Archives Canada

ISBN: 979-8-218-15344-1
Published by Soyounique Press
www.soyounique.ca

Acknowledgement

First, I would like to sincerely thank my entire family for providing me the spiritual and emotional support to put this book together. I want to particularly thank my lovely wife Grace Elimimian for being the prayer backbone and continuously lifting up the family to God in prayers.

Additionally, I would like to thank the Senior Pastor of Arctic for Christ Ministries, Pastor Isaac Omole of blessed memory for the opportunity he granted me to exercise my spiritual gifts at church. I would also like to thank the entire members of Arctic for Christ Ministries for believing and listening to me.

Furthermore, I would like to acknowledge and thank my role model, mentor and friend Dr. Darlington Akaiso for the motivation, inspiration and continuous nudge that culminated partly to the materialization of this book.

Finally, I would like to acknowledge and thank the people that helped to proofread, format and edit the first manuscript. May God that sees whatever is done in the secret reward you all abundantly in the open in Jesus Name.

Dedication

This book is about God's children and their relationship with Jehovah the Almighty God. The book is dedicated to God the Father, the Son and the Holy Spirit.

Foreword

The Book "Significance of the Symbolic" is a practical revelation of what is obtainable in the spiritual realms. Numbers 21:9 describes Jesus' revelation of himself in a story of how "…Moses made a bronze snake and put it up on a pole. Then when anyone was bitten by a snake and looked at the bronze snake, they lived." This invariably means He would be lifted up in the world and anyone that looks unto Him will live.

Everything that exists has spiritual origin. God in his simplistic way has made humans to access the supernatural realm through the simple means of symbols for exploit in the kingdom within.

I find Pastor Francis Elimimian, a man I know from childhood, to have a tremendous grace of divine insights and revelations. I have watched his revelations played out verbatim in times past. I do not personally take Pastor Francis' revelations for granted. I am passionate about the "Significance of the Symbolic" and I have ingested every aspect of the book. As Pastor Francis has scripted the mind of God through the simple means of symbols, and shares his experiences in this book, I will encourage every reader to read, digest and apply this life transforming book to their personal lives.

Pastor Austin Elimimian
Senior Pastor of Tower of Safety Ministry

TABLE OF CONTENT

Introduction

It is a common knowledge in Christian circles that everything in the Old Testament is a shadow of Jesus Christ in the New Testament. There are biblical symbolic representations respected by different Christian denominations. This book is about the revelation I received concerning some biblical symbols handed down from generation to generation of God's people.

At the beginning of the year 2020, I decided to be in the presence of God everyday. I continued fellowshipping with the Lord daily, until one day when I was on a trip from Iqaluit to Ottawa with two of my children who occupied the middle position in our family. While on the aircraft, the Spirit of God came heavily upon me and whispered **"significance of the symbolic,"** to my hearing. As I listened, the Holy Spirit presented me the symbols of faith, oil, temple, communion, and cross, which I wrote down on my phone. All of these happened at 32,000 feet above ground level going by the information given to me by the flight attendant, when I asked her.

Afterwards, I tried to put off the revelation, but the Lord kept bringing it back to me urging me to disseminate the revelation to others. I preached about the revelation in the church I attend, hoping that the promptings to disseminate the revelation will come to an end, but it kept on coming back. Hence, I began to pen down the revelation to share with as many as would be willing to read and apply it.

This book is organised into seven chapters, not according to the order of the revelation, but to have arrangement that facilitate a smooth flow.

The First chapter is the introduction and the circumstances leading to the writing of this book.

Chapter two is about the symbolism of Faith. The bible says

"Now faith is the substance of things hoped for, the evidence of things not seen" Hebrews 11:1 (KJV)

Faith is considered abstract and invisible, but the bible described it as a substance. This book sheds more light on the over-arching questions as to why "Faith" is considered abstract and invisible, and yet referred to as a "substance" in the bible.

Chapter three deals with the revelations about the Oil. The oil is symbolic of the Holy Spirit. The anointing oil is very important in both the old and new testaments. This chapter explores the significance of the anointing oil in the life of the believers. The bible describes the Holy Spirit as a person, who is invisible and yet is present everywhere. This chapter will document the revelation given to me concerning the oil and the Holy Spirit.

Chapter four records the revelation about the temple of God. King Solomon built a magnificent temple for God, then the Temple was destroyed in 586 BC by Nebuchadnezzar, the King of Babylon, at the time conquered Jerusalem and sent Israel into exile. At the release of Israel from captivity, the second temple was erected and completed around 515 BC. Today, we have several magnificent temples for worships. The revelation received about the temple of God is documented in this chapter.

Chapter five is about the Holy Communion. All the four Gospels of Matthew, Mark, Luke and John recorded the account of the Holy Communion. The early apostles practised it, and it is still practised in churches today. The symbolism of the Holy Communion as revealed to me is clearly documented in this chapter.

Chapter six records the revelation of the symbolism of Jesus on the cross. Without the cross would there be salvation? Is the cross of Jesus still relevant in today's world? This sixth chapter answered some of the questions about the cross and its necessity in today's church.

In Chapter seven, the revelation of the Passover was given to me in a separate revelation during the 2020 COVID-19 pandemic that ravaged the whole world. While I was praying to God for protection during the pandemic, the Holy Spirit said to me "Passover! Passover!!" While, I was wondering what the Lord was trying to say to me; I travelled in the spirit to Exodus 12:13 and the Lord says "Now the blood shall be a sign for you on the houses where you are. And when I see the blood, I will pass over you; and the plague shall not be on you too." The Lord implanted in my spirit man the desire to invoke the covenant of the Passover in the blood of Jesus Christ. In fact, this revelation is an extension of the revelation of the communion, but for simplicity and ease of digestion, I decided to write about it in a separate chapter.

Happy Reading

Faith

Chapter 02

"The key that opens all doors"

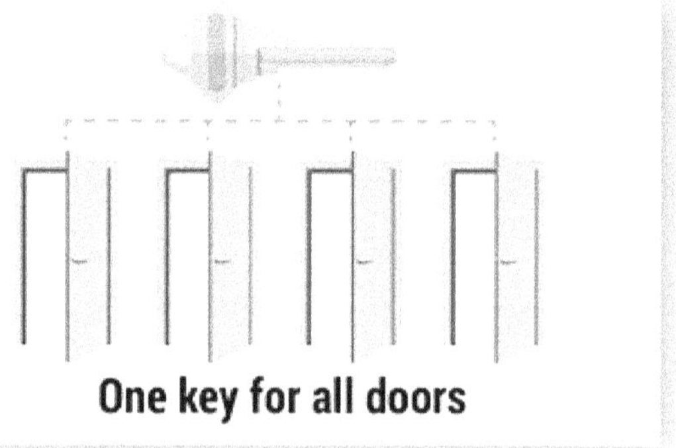

Faith. Lock surgeon master key systems locksmith. (n.d.). Retrieved February 18, 2023, from https://www.locksurgeon.com/master-key-systems-locksmith.php

" Now faith is the substance of things hoped for, the evidence of things not seen"

Hebrews 11:1 (KJV)

FAITH is the first symbol in the series of the symbolic revelation I received from God. The Spirit of God revealed to me that Faith being abstract and invisible is the symbol (concrete evidence) of our beliefs. The Holy Spirit went further to reveal to me that FAITH is the bedrock of the 'beliefs' anyone could ever have in anything: Whether Christian or non-Christian, the Holy Spirit made it expressly clear to me that without faith nothing works.

I had a personal experience, once upon a time, when an organisation that I worked for invited a hypnotist to an event we held. The hypnotist decided to perform his hypnosis on selected volunteers. volunteers came out willingly, and our president/Chief Executive Officer jokingly said "hey Francis join them," to which I replied that hypnotism will not work on me. Anyway, because of my regard for him, I joined them for the hypnotist's exercise. I had no faith in whatever the hypnotist was planning to do. The hypnotist immediately recognized this and after making several moves to which some people responded, he quickly asked me and another guy to go back to our seat.

In the beginning of the Bible God demonstrated FAITH in Himself and created the visible things out of the invisible. God created you and me and endowed us with the same abilities as HIS. But it is only by Faith we can achieve those Godlike abilities in us.

> "¹In the beginning God created the heaven and the earth. ²And the earth was without form, and void; and darkness was upon the face of the deep. And the Spirit of God moved upon the face of the waters. ³And God said, Let there be light: and there was light". Genesis 1:1-3

"So, God created man in His own image, in the image and likeness of God He created him; male and female He created them." Genesis 1:27 (AMP)

God said, **"Let there be light and there was light"** God had and still has faith in himself that when HE speaks a word, it will come to pass as he has spoken. That is why the bible says **"And without faith it is impossible to please God, because anyone who comes to him must believe that he exists and that he rewards those who earnestly seek him"** Hebrews 11:6 (NIV).

The Holy Spirit made me to understand that FAITH is the foundation of the Christian's relationship with the Almighty God. Without FAITH you cannot please God. Without FAITH you cannot get much from God. So, if you want to go far as a Christian or even non-Christian you must understand what I will call **"FAITH 101,"** which is the rudiments of FAITH. At the time I was pursuing my undergraduate studies, all the students admitted straight from High School to study courses such as medicine, accounting, literature, economics, and so on, had to pass through the School of General and Remedial Studies (SGRS), where we took various general courses as well as introductory coursesof major. The names of all the courses offered in that school were appended with the numerical suffix 101, 102 or 103 etcetera. Examples include Algebra 101, Economics 101, Mathematics 101 to mention a few. This school prepared us for a whole year, before dispatching us to our respective departments, programs or faculties. In this like, all Christians must go through Faith 101 preparatory to qualify for victorious Christian living.

As a believer in God, you must realize that He has equipped you with spiritual gifts for your benefit and that of the entire body of Christ. Without faith in God, no one can activate these spiritual gifts:

"[7]But the manifestation of the Spirit is given to every man to profit withal. [8]For to one is given by the Spirit the word of wisdom; to another the word of knowledge by the same Spirit; [9]To another faith by the same Spirit; to another the gifts of healing by the same Spirit; [10]To another the working of miracles; to another prophecy; to another discerning of spirits; to another divers kinds of tongues; to another the interpretation of tongues: [11]But all these worketh that one and the selfsame Spirit, dividing to every man severally as he will" 1Corinth 12:7-11 (KJV).

God has also elected the believers to function in one or more ministries or offices.

"And God hath set some in the church, first apostles, secondarily prophets, thirdly teachers, after that miracles, then gifts of healings, helps, governments, diversities of tongues"
I Corintians 12:28

"[11]And he gave some, apostles; and some, prophets; and some, evangelists; and some, pastors and teachers. [12]For the perfecting of the saints, for the work of the ministry, for the edifying of the body of Christ:" Ephesians 4:11,12 (KJV)

Finally, God expects believers to produce fruits as they mature spiritually:

"So, produce fruit that is consistent with repentance [demonstrating new behavior that proves a change of heart, and a conscious decision to turn away from sin]" Matthew 3:8 (AMP)

It's noteworthy that, a Christian may have little or nothing to do to receive the gifts of the Holy Spirit or elected into one or more of the ministry offices, but a Christian has much to do to bring forth Fruits. However, none of these can happen without faith.

It is, therefore, imperative for every Christian to start with the knowledge of FAITH 101 to prepare themselves to have a victorious walk with God. As a young convert in the Assemblies of God (AG) church in my teenage years; first, I passed through the "Enquirer's class" for a couple of months, where I received preparatory trainings about the Holy Trinity, Faith and the Assemblies of God doctrines. Next, I was elevated to the baptismal class that culminated into water baptism by immersion. By Faith I was baptised in the Holy Ghost before my water baptism. Since then my life has never been the same. God has taken me to places, availed me of unspeakable opportunities, elevated me and showed me revelations that cannot be uttered by words of mouth or documented in this book.

From a revelation I received, Noah was a regular man like other folks in his generation; he lived where others lived, he ate the same food as others and was engaged in a similar profession as his counterparts. But he had Faith in God unlike others. This made God to trust Noah and reveal His mind to him. The bible has no record of rainfall before then, but God revealed to Noah that it was going to rain and that the whole world was going to be destroyed by the flood from the rainfall.

"And, behold, I, even I, do bring a flood of waters upon the earth, to destroy all flesh, wherein is the breath of life, from under heaven; and everything that is in the earth shall die" Genesis 6:17 (KJV). God also revealed a prototype of the Ark to Noah to build to save himself, his family and of every living thing of all flesh, male and female to keep them alive.

The bible says by Faith Noah believed and obeyed. He built the Ark and went in with his family and all other things in accordance with God's instructions.

The Holy Spirit brought this home for me when he took me to the circles of the meteorologists predicting impending extreme and disastrous weather conditions such hurricanes, tsunamis, storms and tornados but unable to improvise remedy to avert the disaster. However, God is not like the meteorologists, God reveals to save.

Jesus said to Peter

"[31] … Simon, Simon, behold, Satan hath desired to have you, that he may sift you as wheat: [32]But I have prayed for thee, that thy faith fail not: and when thou art converted, strengthen thy brethren" Luke 22:31, 32 (KJV).

Imagine how it would have felt, if the Lord had revealed that Hurricane Katrina was going to happen at the time it did, and the Lord also revealing to you what to do to avert the hurricane. Then, while the meteorologist would be predicting the impending hurricane, you would come forth to declare the word of the Lord and all that is needed to avert the impeding hurricane, to the glory of the Lord's name.

Or, think about anything you consider impossible in your personal life, family or your environment, and how you will feel to approach it by Faith and see it becoming possible. In my personal life, by Faith I have had countless experiences of God turning impossibilities to possibilities.

Abraham (that was called Abram) lived among his kindred. He enjoyed life with his family, siblings and relatives, he had challenges like others but above all he had Faith in God. Then one day, God spoke to Abram to arise and depart from his parents, siblings, relatives and from all his kindred to an unknown place.

"Now the Lord had said unto Abram, Get thee out of thy country, and from thy kindred, and from thy father's house, unto a land that I will shew thee" Genesis 12:1 (KJV)

By Faith Abraham believed God and it was counted for him as righteousness.

> "And he believed in the Lord; and he counted it to him for righteousness"
> Genesis 15:6

The Holy Spirit reminded me that achievement of his full potentials in God depended largely on Faith. Therefore, if you and I want to attain our full potentials we must learn to walk with God by Faith. Walking with God by Faith could be construed to be stupidity or foolishness by the world, but in the end, you will come out honourably. The bible says the carnal man does not understand the things of the Spirit

> "But the natural man receiveth not the things of the Spirit of God: for they are foolishness unto him: neither can he know them, because they are spiritually discerned" I Corinthians 2:14 (KJV).

Shadrach, Meshach and Abednego had Faith in God and said to King Nebuchadnezzar that they will never worship his idol:

> "[17]If it be so, our God whom we serve is able to deliver us from the burning fiery furnace, and he

will deliver us out of thine hand, O king. [18] But if not, be it known unto thee, O king, that we will not serve thy gods, nor worship the golden image which thou hast set up" Daniel 3:17-18 (KJV).

Faith is in different categories and faith is needed in every aspect of our lives. Jesus Christ spoke about little Faith that was exemplified with limitations. Therefore, as believers destined for victorious living, we must nurture our Faith in God to develop, and apply FAITH in different dimensions and diverse circumstances.

There came a tempest and contrary wind blowing against the disciples of Jesus Christ and they were afraid, but Jesus said to them:

"...why are ye fearful, O ye of little faith? Then he arose, and rebuked the winds and the sea; and there was a great calm" Matthew 8:26 (KJV)

If you are going through any tempest and your Faith is waning, pray to God to increase your Faith and rebuke the tempest by faith.

Have you started anything by faith and oppositions began to rise from all directions, from close friends, family or colleagues, from the Government or institutions, that you began to entertain fear…of losing, fear of litigation or disciplinary action? I want you to realize that you cannot fail nor perish, and you cannot go back from where you were, but you can only go forward with your Faith in Christ; so, cry out to JESUS to help you and to increase your Faith.

> "²⁹And he said, Come. And when Peter was come down out of the ship, he walked on the water, to go to Jesus. ³⁰But when he saw the wind boisterous, he was afraid; and beginning to sink, he cried, saying, Lord, save me. ³¹And immediately Jesus stretched forth his hand, and caught him, and said unto him, O thou of little faith, wherefore didst thou doubt?"
> Matthew 14:29-31 (KJV)

A man brought his son that had a problem of seizures to Jesus' disciples and they could not heal him. Thanks be to God that Jesus came in the nick of time and healed the sick. Afterwards, the disciple went to ask Jesus, "why could we not heal him?" Jesus answered them…." because of your little faith." The disciples needed to pray to increase their Faith.

> He said to them, "Because of your little faith. For truly, I say to you, if you have faith as a grain of

mustard seed, you will say to this mountain, 'Move from here to there,' and it will move; and nothing will be impossible to you" Matthew 17:20 (RSV)

Believers need Faith to save themselves from worry, anxiety and depression. Before, I started the university for my undergraduate studies, there already existed a considerably high level of unemployment among university graduates. After my final year, I was a graduate intern, very worried and losing sleeps at night, thinking about how I could be employed. During one of those days, I was at a motor park and multitude of passengers was waiting, and I was anxious again. The Spirit of God spoke to me, did you consider the woman of Revelation Chapter twelve, how she was to put forth to birth and the dragon was waiting to devour her and the baby once born? But when the baby was born, power from above snatched him away and the woman escaped to a place that God had prepared for her. Then, the spirit of the Lord said to me, I will snatch you away from the market of unemployment and give you the job I have prepared for you. That was exactly how it happened.

"[4]...and the dragon stood before the woman, which was ready to be delivered, for to devour her child as soon as it was born. [5]And she brought forth a man child, who was to rule all nations with a rod of iron: and her child was caught up unto God, and to his throne. ⁶And the woman fled into the wilderness, where she hath a place prepared of God, that they should feed her there a thousand two hundred and threescore days" Revelation 12:4-6 (KJV)

God is so generous and assures us of caring for us like he does to his other creations like the flowers, the birds and even grass
"²⁷Consider the lilies how they grow: they toil not, they spin not; and yet I say unto you, that Solomon in all his glory was not arrayed like one of these. ²⁸If then God so clothe the grass, which is today in the field, and tomorrow is cast into the oven; how much more will he clothe you, O ye of little faith?"
Luke 12:27-28 (KJV)

Moreover, you need FAITH for wholeness to enjoy the fullness of God in spirit, soul and body. It does not matter whether you are a woman or a man that needs healing or knows someone who does; FAITH brings healing. FAITH can heal you of every sickness be it physical, emotional, social, spiritual or financial. Just reach out to Jesus by FAITH.

"And Jesus answered them, truly, I say to you, if you have faith and do not doubt, you will not only do what has been done to the fig tree, but even if you say to this mountain, 'Be taken up and thrown into the sea,' it will happen. And whatever you ask in prayer, you will receive, if you have faith." Matthew 21:21-22

Faith is the medicine you need to be whole. A woman that suffered issue of blood for twelve years and was seen by numerous doctors to no avail, touched Jesus by FAITH and she was healed instantaneously.

"But Jesus turned him about, and when he saw her, he said, Daughter, be of good comfort; thy faith hath made thee whole. And the woman was made whole from that hour." Matthew 9:22(KJV)

Another woman came by FAITH to Jesus on behalf of her daughter and her daughter was made whole.

Then Jesus answered and said unto her, O woman, great is thy faith: be it unto thee even as thou wilt. And her daughter was made whole from that very hour" Matthew 15:28 (KJV).

Bartimaeus cried out to Jesus by FAITH and he was healed.

"And Jesus said unto him, Go thy way; thy faith hath made thee whole. And immediately he received his sight and followed Jesus in the way" Mark 10:52.

Christian needs Faith for sanctification, by faith in Jehovah Mekoddishkem you shall be cleansed of all impurities including infirmities

"[8]God, who knows the heart, showed that he accepted them by giving the Holy Spirit to them, just as he did to us. [9]He did not discriminate between us and them, for he purified their hearts by faith." Acts 15:8-9 (NIV)

Faith is needed for Christians' day to day living

"[16] For I am not ashamed of the gospel of Christ: for it is the power of God unto salvation to everyone that believeth; to the Jew first, and also to the Greek. [17] For therein is the righteousness of God revealed from faith to faith: as it is written, The just shall live by faith.." Romans 1:16-17

Finally, by Faith we are raised together with Jesus Christ and seated on the right hand side of God. These are privileges we can only realise if we have unwavering faith in God. The bible says

"[13]We having the same spirit of faith, according as it is written, I believed, and therefore have I spoken; we also believe, and therefore speak; [14]Knowing that he which raised up the Lord Jesus shall raise up us also by Jesus, and shall present us with you." 2 Corinthians 4:13-14 (KJV)

Oil

Chapter 03

Oil background. iStock. (n.d.). Retrieved February 18, 2023, from
https://www.istockphoto.com/photo/drop-on-the-oil-gm504828464-83360269

The revelation of the anointing oil as symbolic of the Holy Spirit will be discussed with emphasis on the Holy Spirit, and then the revelation around the anointing oil will be unveiled.

Now the Holy Spirit is the third person in the triune God (Father, Son and the Holy Spirit). The Holy Spirit has been with God since the beginning of creation.

"[1]In the beginning God created the heaven and the earth. [2] And the earth was without form, and void; and darkness was upon the face of the deep. And the Spirit of God moved upon the face of the waters" Gen 1:1,2 (KJV)

The Hebrew word "RUACH" is what was translated as Spirit in the above scriptures and as "wind" or "breath" throughout the Old Testament.

"By His breath the heavens are cleared…." Job 26:13

Moreover, at the creation of man the bible says

"And the LORD God formed man of the dust of the ground, and breathed into his nostrils the breath of life; and man became a living soul" Gen 2:7 (KJV).

In the very beginning, God created the heaven and the earth, but the bible says

"And the earth was without form, and void; and darkness was upon the face of the deep, And the Spirit of God moved upon the face of the waters" (Gen 1:2).

Here the Earth that was just created by God the father and the son (Word) was without form, void and full of darkness. Then, God the Spirit began to move upon the surface of the waters providing semblance, fullness and light to the newly created heaven and Earth.

Again, in Gen 2:7 God formed man out of the dust of the earth, and man was nothing but a sculpture. According to the bible, God breathed (ruach) into his nostrils the breath of life; and man became a living soul. Therefore, it was by the making of the Holy Spirit that man became a living soul.

Redemption of humanity was also accomplished through the Spirit of God.

> Jesus answered, Verily, verily, I say unto thee, Except a man be born of water and of the Spirit, he cannot enter into the kingdom of God" John 3:5 (KJV).

The Holy Spirit is very important throughout the Old and New Testaments of the Bible, as well as today in the entire universe. But the modus operandi of the Holy Spirit in the old testament is totally different from His modus operandi in our current dispensation. In the Old Testament, it took a prophet to prophesy about the outpouring of the Holy Spirit in the later days to come.

> "And it shall come to pass afterward, that I will pour out my spirit upon all flesh; and your sons and your daughters shall prophesy, your old men shall dream dreams, your young men shall see visions:"
> Joel:2:28 (KJV)

The Holy Spirit was not available to everyone from the very beginning, it took Joel in his days to prophesy about the future abundance of the Holy Spirit In all, the Holy Spirit is vital and needed in all noble endeavours throughout the universe. In the old testament, the power of the Holy Spirit rested mostly on the prophets and seers and at some point on craftsmen like Bezalel (Exodus 31). In the old testament, the Kings worked with the Priests and the Prophets. The Holy Spirit was needed to carry out assigned responsibilities. God always transfer the power of the Holy Spirit himself or sometimes, He may ask the priest to anoint or lay hands on a person and the Holy Spirit would come directly from God upon the person assigned with new responsibility.

"And the Lord came down in a cloud, and spake unto him, and took of the spirit that was upon him, and gave it unto the seventy elders: and it came to pass, that, when the spirit rested upon them, they prophesied, and did not cease." Numbers 11:25 (KJV).

When the seventy elders were chosen to assist Moses with leadership and administrative responsibilities to the people of Israel, God himself transferred a portion of the Holy Spirit in Moses upon the people to enable them carry out their duties.

Before the first monarch (King Saul) was appointed in Israel, Samuel the High Priest anointed him with oil and gave him instructions.

> "[1]Then Samuel took a vial of oil, and poured it upon his head, and kissed him, and said, Is it not because the LORD hath anointed thee to be captain over his inheritance? [5]And the Spirit of the LORD will come upon thee, and thou shalt prophesy with them, and shalt be turned into another man" ISamuel 10:1, 5 (KJV).

By God's special instruction, Elijah called Elisha to become his successor and Elijah transferred the Holy Spirit upon Elisha. Elisha so much enjoyed his encounters with the Holy Spirit that in the end when Elijah asked Elisha to ask him of anything, all that Elisha could ask for was a double (another) portion of the Holy Spirit.

> "And it came to pass, when they had gone over, that Elijah said unto Elisha, "Ask what I shall do for thee, before I be taken away from thee." And Elisha

said, "I pray thee, let a double portion of thy spirit be upon me." 2 Kings 2:9 (KJV)

Jesus Christ could not start His ministry on Earth until after the Holy Spirit has come upon Him

"And Jesus, when he was baptized, went up straightway out of the water: and, lo, the heavens were opened unto him, and he saw the Spirit of God descending like a dove, and lighting upon him" Matthew 3:16 (KJV)

When Jesus was about to leave the earth, He re-informed the disciples about the Holy Spirit and how important He is. Here, Jesus was telling His disciples about his imminent departure. The disciples became worried and sad. Then Jesus said to them, if you love me and keep my commandments, I will pray to God the father to send you another (like me) comforter. Jesus went on to tell the disciples, that the comforter (the Holy Spirit) will remind them everything he has told them. The comforter will teach them everything He (Jesus) has not taught them.

"But the Comforter, which is the Holy Ghost, whom the Father will send in my name, he shall teach you all things, and bring all things to your remembrance, whatsoever I have said unto you" John 14:26 (KJV)

At occasions before Jesus Christ was crucified, after His resurrection and before ascending to Heaven, he emphatically instructed His disciples to tarry in Jerusalem until they were endued by the Holy Spirit from above (Heaven).

"Listen carefully: I am sending the Promise of My Father [the Holy
   Spirit] upon you; but you are to remain in the city
   [of Jerusalem] until you are clothed (fully equipped)
    with power from on high." Luke 24:49 (AMP)

"But ye shall receive power, after that the Holy
Ghost is come upon you: and ye shall be witnesses
unto me both in Jerusalem, and in all Judaea, and in
Samaria, and unto the uttermost part of the earth"
Acts 1:8 (KJV)

Finally, in the upper room where one hundred and twenty followers of Jesus Christ tarried in Jerusalem, the Holy Spirit came upon them and they were transformed.

" ^{2}And suddenly there came a sound from heaven as of a rushing mighty wind, and it filled all the house where they were sitting.3And there appeared unto them cloven tongues like as of fire, and it sat upon each of them.4And they were all filled with the Holy Ghost, and began to speak with other tongues, as the Spirit gave them utterance" Acts 2:2-4 KJV)

Through the power of the Holy Spirit, the disciples were able to do exploits for the cause of Christianity. With reference to Apostle Peter, he was the man that denied Jesus Christ before the crucifixion. But after the Holy Ghost came upon him, he was empowered and emboldened to witness for Christ.

"^{69} Now Peter sat without in the palace: and a damsel came unto him, saying, Thou also wast with Jesus of Galilee.^{70} But he denied before them all, saying, I know not what thou sayest. ^{71} And when he was gone out into the porch, another maid saw him, and said unto them that were there, This fellow was also with Jesus of Nazareth. ^{72} And again he denied with an oath, I do not know the man. ^{73} And after a while came unto him they that stood by, and said to Peter, Surely thou also art one of them; for thy speech bewrayeth thee. ^{74} Then began he to curse and to swear, saying, I know not the man. And immediately the cock crew." Matthew 26: 69-74 (KJV)

Immediately after the Holy Ghost experience in the upper room on that fateful Pentecost Sunday, the inhabitants and visitors to Jerusalem accused the disciples of being drunken, but Peter being filled with the Holy Ghost addressed the crowd, of which three thousand men (besides women and children) listened and converted to Christ Jesus

"[40]And with many other words did he testify and exhort, saying, Save yourselves from this untoward generation.[41] Then they that gladly received his word were baptized: and the same day there were added unto them about three thousand souls" Acts 2:40-41 (KJV)

In the early apostolic church after the ascension of Jesus Christ, the Holy Spirit was actively involved in strengthening the church and helping the early Christians. The help of the Holy Spirit was very fundamental to the survival of the Christians in withstanding the storms of opposition, resentment and rejection. These resulted in some of them being martyred.

In the book of Acts, the Apostles performed a noticeable miracle at the gate of the Temple in the name of Jesus by the power of the Holy Spirit. Afterwards, the disciples were summoned to the Jewish Council comprised of the priests, the captain of the temple, and the Sadducees. They were cross-examined to perhaps find grounds to prosecute, incarcerate or execute them. Finding no reasons to convict the Apostles, the council flogged and forbade them from ever speaking to anyone about Jesus Christ and his resurrection. Consequently, the disciples were intimidated, depressed and feeling disillusioned.

But the disciples came back to their own Christian folks and debriefed them about the notable miracle, their arraignment by the council and subsequent ordeal. This caused the Christians to lift their voices and pray unto God and the Holy Spirit came down. They became strengthened and continued to speak the word of God and speak about the resurrection of Jesus Christ with boldness.

" [31] And when they had prayed, the place was shaken where they were assembled together; and they were all filled with the Holy Ghost, and they spake the word of God with boldness. [33] And with great power gave the apostles witness of the resurrection of the Lord Jesus: and great grace was upon them all" Acts 4:31 & 33 (KJV).

Some references have been made to the inevitability of the Holy Spirit in the life of the Children of God. Personally, I have been a Christian all my life and I have been filled with the Holy Spirit for over 30 years. I have experienced striking differences between my pre and post Holy Spirit filled Christian life. First, there's no Christian without a measure of the Holy Ghost, but every Christian needs a higher measure than the measure of the Holy Spirit needed to confess Jesus Christ as Lord and the son of God.

" Wherefore I give you to understand, that no man speaking by the Spirit of God calleth Jesus accursed: and that no man can say that Jesus is the Lord, but by the Holy Ghost" I Corinthians 12:3 (KJV).

It was quite frustrating when I was coveting to be filled by the Holy Ghost power. As a child, I attended a denomination where the Holy Spirit was not emphasized. I was growing up with great zeal for God but with little or no knowledge. In the first half of my high school I thought I was cool: Smoking, drinking alcohol and actively searching for girls to befriend. But in my penultimate class in the high school I met one brother Stanley Okoduwa who presented Christ to me in a different way that I was not accustomed to. I started accompanying him to the church where he worshipped, where much emphasis was placed on the Holy Spirit and the benefit of being filled with the Holy Spirit. Eventually, I became born again and that was the beginning of my search for the baptism of the Holy Spirit.

I searched for the baptism of the Holy Ghost for five years, yes! The whole of five years. It was tough for me as a young Christian who was not yet baptised in the Holy Ghost. Finally, I was filled with the Holy Ghost and began to speak in tongues. It was like a heavy weight had been lifted off my head and my shoulders, and I began to enjoy Christianity. Perhaps, as you are reading this book, if you desire the baptism of the Holy Spirit or know someone who does, then I have good news for you because you are seeking a good thing. Secondly, in this dispensation of time, God has poured out the spirit upon all flesh, therefore you are eligible to be filled by the Holy Ghost.

"And it shall come to pass afterward, that I will pour out my spirit upon all flesh; and your sons and your daughters shall prophesy, your old men shall dream dreams, your young men shall see visions"
Joel 2:28

The "Anointing Oil" symbolises the Holy Spirit. It is noteworthy that the infilling of the Holy Spirit is not a one-off event, but a continuous one. Therefore, whether you are already filled or are still seeking to be filled by the Holy Spirit, I strongly recommend anointing yourself as often as you can, desist from engaging in things that will drive the holy spirit away from you, then you will continue to enjoy the presence of the Holy Spirit.

The Efficacy of the anointing oil was demonstrated in the life of the first two kings of Israel.

" [1]Then Samuel took a vial of oil, and poured it upon his head, and kissed him, and said, Is it not because the Lord hath anointed thee to be captain over his inheritance? [10]And when they came thither to the hill, behold, a company of prophets met him; and the Spirit of God came upon him, and he prophesied among them" I Samuel 10:1 -10 (KJV)

.

"Then Samuel took the horn of oil, and anointed him in the midst of his brethren: and the Spirit of the Lord came upon David from that day forward. So Samuel rose up, and went to Ramah" I Samuel 16:13 (KJV).

Samuel anointing Saul with the oil resulted in five unique virtues being released to Saul. They include the hearing of Good News, experiencing favour, getting a New Heart, receiving a New Ability and kingship.

Good News – Saul was just so miserable looking for his father's missing ass. He had gone from one place to another looking for the ass until his encounter with Samuel, which culminated in being anointed by him. After the anointing Samuel told Saul that he will see a set of two men that will share good news with him about the asses that had been found, and how his father was now worried about his whereabouts.

"When thou art departed from me today, then thou shalt find two men by Rachel's sepulchre in the border of Benjamin at Zelzah; and they will say unto thee, The asses which thou wentest to seek are found: and, lo, thy father hath left the care of the asses, and sorroweth for you, saying, What shall I do for my son?" I Samuel 10:2

Favour – Samuel went on to inform Saul that favour has followed him. As an evidence, Samuel informed Saul that he will find three men that will look favourably upon him and give him gifts.

" ³Then shalt thou go on forward from thence, and thou shalt come to the plain of Tabor, and there shall meet thee three men going up to God to Bethel, one carrying three kids, and another carrying three loaves of bread, and another carrying a bottle of wine: 4And they will salute thee, and give thee two loaves of bread; which thou shalt receive of their hands" I Samuel 10:3 - 4.

Jesus Christ was an example of a man that was full of the Holy Spirit and the bible says Jesus found favour with God and with men. If you are looking for favour then you need the infilling and the presence of the Holy Spirit

"And Jesus increased in wisdom and stature, and in favour with God and man" Luke 2:52 (KJV)

New Heart – Saul received a new heart after Samuel anointed him with the oil.

"And it was so, that when he had turned his back to go from Samuel, God gave him another heart: and all those signs came to pass that day" I Samuel 10:9 (KJV).

The oil is symbolic of the Holy Spirit. If you want your heart to be transformed to conform to the standard of God, then you need the Holy Spirit. If you need any heart regeneration or transplant, the Holy Spirit is waiting to help you. So, seek to receive the baptism of the Holy Spirit, even as you continue to anoint yourself with the anointing oil.

New Ability – Following the pouring of the oil upon Saul a new level of abilities rested upon him. Saul met a group of prophets that were prophesying, and the Holy Spirit stirred in him up the ability to prophesy within him and Saul who had never prophesied joined the company of the prophets and began to prophesy so that the onlookers began to question if Saul was also among the prophets.

[10]And when they came thither to the hill, behold, a company of prophets met him; and the Spirit of God came upon him, and he prophesied among them. [11]And it came to pass, when all that knew him before time saw that, behold, he prophesied among the prophets, then the people said one to another,

What is this that is come unto the son of Kish? Is Saul also among the prophets? I Samuel 10:10 - 11 (KJV)

If you need new abilities to do the things you have never done before or things you never imagine you could do, then you need the anointing.

Kingship – The most remarkable thing about the anointing of Saul was that he became a king. Before then, there had never been a king in Israel neither was there any evidence of kingship in the lineage of Saul. So, if you are contemplating something that has not been done in your lineage before, then the anointing of the Holy Spirit upon you can deliver whatever it is to you.

Then Samuel took a vial of oil, and poured it upon his head, and kissed him, and said, Is it not because the Lord hath anointed thee to be captain over his inheritance?" I Samuel 10:1 (KJV)

Every Christian inevitably needs the partnership of the Holy Spirit to succeed in all their endeavours. Anointing yourself constantly will always keep you within the aura of the Holy Spirit. This will be your take home from the revelation of Oil as symbolic of the Holy Spirit.

Temple

AncientPages.com. (2020, January 16). Mystery of king Solomon's temple. Ancient Pages. Retrieved February 18, 2023, from
https://www.ancientpages.com/2018/12/03/mystery-of-king-solomons-temple/

"Know ye not that ye are the temple of God,
and that the Spirit of God dwelleth in you?" I
Corinthians 3:16 (KJV)

The temple is analogous of the tabernacle, while the tabernacle was a temporary structure, the temple was a more permanent structure. Throughout the Bible, the Temple was used as a house of God where God's presence resides. The reference to Temple received prominence at the beginning of Israel's Monarchy (rulership by kings). First, the bible reports how the people of Israel were visiting the Temple of God at Shiloh once every year to hear from God. In one of those visits to Shiloh, Hannah who had been barren prayed, promising God that if He will give her a son, she will offer him to be in God's service all of his life.

"⁹So Hannah rose up after they had eaten in Shiloh, and after they had drunk. Now Eli the priest sat upon a seat by a post of the temple of the LORD. ¹⁰And she was in bitterness of soul, and prayed unto the LORD, and wept sore. ¹¹And she vowed a vow, and said, O LORD of hosts, if thou wilt indeed look on the affliction of thine handmaid, and remember me, and not forget thine handmaid, but wilt give unto thine handmaid a man child, then I will give him unto the LORD all the days of his life, and there shall no razor come upon his head" (I Samuel I:9-11)

God granted Hannah's request and in fulfilment of her pledge, when Hannah gave birth to her son, whom she named Samuel, in fulfillment of her pledge, she brought him to the Temple in Shiloh, which they believed is the house of God, where Samuel lived under the priesthood of Eli

"And ere the lamp of God went out in the temple of the LORD, where the ark of God was, and Samuel was laid down to sleep" ISamuel 3:3

The presence of the Ark of God was mentioned here in addition to the presence of God in the temple. The Temple of God was hallowed and revered. King David wanted to build a Temple, but God forbade him because there was too much human blood on his hands. King David however made arrangements for his son Solomon, who built the Temple in his father's stead, when he became King. In his prayers at the Temple's dedication Solomon emphasized the presence of God in the Temple. I have surely built thee an house to dwell in, a settled place for thee to abide in for ever" IKings8:13

The word "Temple" was mentioned a few times in the bible before the Temple of Solomon, but the Temple Solomon built was mostly referred as the first Temple in biblical conversation. It was the first of its kind, a magnificently erected edifice meant to replicate the elements of the tabernacle in greater dimensions. The Temple like the tabernacle consisted of different courts.

The temple of Solomon and its courts. Bible Odyssey. (2022, December 12). Retrieved February 18, 2023, from https://www.bibleodyssey.org/image-gallery/the-temple-of-solomon-and-its-courts/

Heinrich Bünting, The Temple of Solomon and Its Courts, 1585. From Itinerarium Sacrae Scripturae, part 1 (Helmstadt: Jacobus Lucius, 1585), 34–35. Jewish National and University Library, Hebrew University of Jerusalem, Israel.

Outermost Court or later Court of the Gentiles: The outermost court was the outside area of the temple in Jerusalem and was called the court of the Gentiles, where everyone could enter. It was the most exterior and, by far, the largest of all the courts. This location, along with Solomon's Porch (which was a covered area that existed on either side of the court's eastern entrance was frequented by Jerusalem's sick folks and the poor seeking help (Acts 3:11, 5:12, 15).

The Outer Court (The Court of the Women and the Court of Israel): The outer court was next to the outermost court where all of Israel had access to.

"And the porch before the temple of the house, twenty cubits was the length thereof, according to the breadth of the house; and ten cubits was the breadth thereof before the house" I Kings 6:3 (KJV)

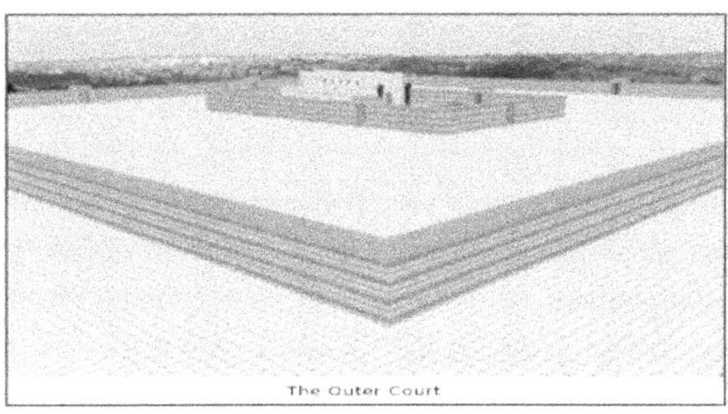

The Outer Court. Bible history. (n.d.). Retrieved February 18, 2023, from http://bible-history.com/

The outer court consist of the Court of Women and the Court of Israel.

The Court of the Women was considered the place where Israeli women could worship God in Jerusalem's Temple. Females could not go beyond this point into the court of Israel unless they were bringing a sacrifice. It was the place where sacrificial animals were bought, foreign currency was exchanged for sacred money, and it was where sacrificial doves could be purchased by the poor. This was where Jesus Christ overthrew the tables of the money changers.

And Jesus went into the temple of God, and cast out all them that sold and bought in the temple, and overthrew the tables of the moneychangers, and the seats of them that sold doves" Matthew 21:12 (KJV)

The Court of Israel, which was open to Jewish laymen is next to the court of women. There were three gates on both the south and the north sides, making seven entrances in all. Eleven cubits of the eastern end were partitioned off by a stone balustrade, one cubit high, for the men, separating it from the rest of the space that formed the court of the priests.

The Court of the Priests or Holy Place: The Holy place is the court after the outer court and before the Inner sanctuary (the Holy of holies). The measurement of the Holy Place in Solomon's temple was forty cubits (sixty feet) long, twenty cubits (thirty feet) wide and thirty cubits (forty five feet) high. Everything inside the Temple was either made of pure gold or overlaid with gold. The furniture of the Holy Place consisted of ten golden lampstands, five on the right side and five on the left; also, ten tables of showbread, five on the right side and five on the left.

"[17]The house, that is, the main room in front of the inner sanctuary, was forty cubits long. [18]There was cedar inside the house, carved in the shape of gourds and open flowers; everything was cedar, there was no stone visible" I Kings 6:17, 18 (KJV)

The Holy Place. Bible history. (n.d.). Retrieved February 18, 2023, from http://bible-history.com/

The Holy Place was the court of the priests. Inside the holy place the priests would discharge various duties as representatives of the people of Israel before God. Firstly, they would offer incense on the golden-incense altar, burn sweet-smelling incense every morning and evening. The smoke from the incense rose to the ceiling, went through the opening above the veil, and filled the Holy of Holies during the high priest's annual rites. Secondly, the priests will place twelve loaves of unleavened bread, representing the twelve tribes of Israel on the table in the Holy Place. The bread was usually eaten and replaced every Sabbath day by the priests inside the Holy Place. Thirdly, they will also tend the golden lampstand, or menorah, that illuminates the Holy Place throughout the year.

The Court of the High Priest (The Most Holy Place or Holy of Holies): The Holy of holies is the innermost court of the Temple that existed within the Holy Place of the tabernacle (temple). The Holy of Holies, or the Most Holy Place when originally constructed by King Solomon as a replica of the holy of holies in the tabernacle was twenty cubits, by twenty cubits, by twenty cubits. It was a cube. The most holy place was entirely overlaid with pure gold (twenty four (24) karats) and believed to be where God's presence resides in the temple.

"And the oracle in the forepart was twenty cubits in
length, and twenty cubits in breadth, and twenty
cubits in the height thereof: and he overlaid it with
pure gold; and so covered the altar which was of
cedar." I Kings 6:20.

The contents of the most holy place are the golden censer and the ark of the Covenant wherein was the golden pot that had manna, Aaron's rod that budded, and the tables of the covenant (twelve commandments).

"Which had the golden censer, and the ark of the
covenant overlaid round about with gold, wherein
was the golden pot that had manna, and Aaron's rod
that budded, and the tables of the covenant"
Hebrews 9:4 (KJV)

The most Holy Place. Bible history. (n.d.). Retrieved February 18, 2023, from http://bible-history.com/

Only the High Priest went into the Most Holy Place once in a year. Any High Priest that entered the Most Holy Place unworthily died. Therefore, the High Priest prepared himself thoroughly and performed various sacrifices for himself and Israel before venturing into the Most Holy Place to make atonement for himself and Israel as a whole.

"but into the second [inner tabernacle, the Holy of Holies], only the high priest enters [and then only] once a year, and never without [bringing a sacrifice of] blood, which he offers [as a substitutionary atonement] for himself and for the sins of the people committed in ignorance" Hebrews 9:7 (AMP).

The revelation about the Temple: The author was very excited about the revelation of the symbolic of the Temple. We have been talking about the Temple since the beginning of this chapter. The Temple is acclaimed to be the house of God. The temple has various courts and elements for different purposes. But the most significant part of the temple is the holy of holies. That's the place that God's presence resides in the Temple. From the very beginning the contents of the holy of holies are the golden censer, and the ark of the covenant overlaid round about with gold, wherein was the golden pot that had manna, and Aaron's rod that budded, and the tables of the covenant (Hebrews 9:4 - KJV)

The Temple has graduated from various stages as Moses Tabernacle to permanent edifices like the Solomon's Temple (1st Temple), and Herod's Temple (2nd Temple) etcetera. But the most important element of the Temple is the Holy of Holies that represented where the presence of God dwelt.
In the present dispensation in which we live, God does not "dwell" in the temple made by man anymore.

"God that made the world and all things therein, seeing that he is Lord of heaven and earth, dwelleth not in temples made with hands" Acts 17:24 (KJV)

We humans have become the Temple of God where his presence now resides.

> "Know ye not that ye are the temple of God, and that the Spirit of God dwelleth in you?" I Corinthians 3:16 (KJV)

By divine revelation that means the Holy of Holies is now within us, as well as the golden censer and the ark of the covenant containing the pot of the manna, Aaron's rod and the tables of the commandments with its golden lid, the kapporet (translated as "mercy seat" or "cover") covered with two golden cherubim,

In the Revelation of the Symbolic:

(I) **The Golden Censer in the Holy of Holies** used on the day of Atonement were of gold, and was denoted by a word (mahtah) meaning "something to take fire with;" The angel in the Apocalypse is represented as having a golden censer with the prayers of God's people (Revelation 8:3) which means we have the fire of God and prayers incubated within us as people of God.

(2) **The Ark of the Covenant** is symbolic of us (humans) meeting with God. God hovered over the Ark when the priests were present. If the priests were absent, the tablets of the commandments in the Ark reflected God's presence. Thus, since we have

become the Temple of God, we continuously enjoy the eternal presence of God. Moreover, the lid of the Ark "Kapporet" means mercy seat which implies that the mercy of God resides within us.

**(3)		The Pot of Manna:** The presence of the pot of manna within the ark which is now within us symbolizes God's constant provision for us His people. Therefore, we will never be in want of what to eat anymore.

**(4)		Aaron's rod** symbolizes God's Authority and approval now bestowed upon us.

"Having therefore, brethren, boldness to enter into the holiest by the blood of Jesus, 20 By a new and living way, which he hath consecrated for us, through the veil, that is to say, his flesh; 21 And having an high priest over the house of God; 22 Let us draw near with a true heart in full assurance of faith, having our hearts sprinkled from an evil conscience, and our bodies washed with pure water" Hebrews 10:19–22 (KJV)

In summary, the presence of God in the temple (us) is an assurance of victory in every endeavour, this needs to be proclaimed by unwavering faith in God.

Communion

Sermoveritas. (2011, July 13). Sermo Veritas on Tumblr. Tumblr. Retrieved February 18, 2023, from https://www.tumblr.com/sermoveritas

The Holy Communion, Eucharist or the Lord's Supper is a Christian ritual instituted by Jesus Christ in the last evening before His betrayal, and arrest. At the last supper, Jesus gave bread and wine to His disciple as being symbolic of His body and blood and commanded them to continue the ritual in commemoration of Him until He returns, during His second coming.

Jesus set the stage for the Holy Communion before it happened. Jesus performed many miracles, including healing from diverse illnesses and deliverance from evil spirits, making multitudes of people follow him.

"And a great multitude followed him, because they
saw his miracles which he did on them that were
diseased."
– John 6:2 (KJV)

In Jesus' tradition of compassion, he began to teach the
people and engaged them until late in the evening. The
disciples wanted to send the people home to go find their
super, but Jesus said 'no' we can't send them away hungry,
let's give them something to eat. Then Jesus fed them.
The number of people that were fed was five thousand
(5,000) men, beside women and children.

"[20]And they did all eat, and were filled: and they
took up of the fragments that remained twelve
baskets full. [21]And they that had eaten were about
five thousand men, beside women and children."
Matthew 14:20, 21 (KJV)

After the people had eaten and were filled, they were
convinced that Jesus is the type of leader they needed, a
leader that understands, cares and provides for the needs
of their followers. So, the people plotted to forcefully
crown Jesus as their king.

"When Jesus therefore perceived that they would
come and take him by force, to make him a king, he

departed again into a mountain himself alone”
- John 6:15 (KJV)

The multitude of people followed Jesus unto the mountain again. At that point, Jesus said to them, you are following me not because of my teaching but because of the bread, of which, you will eat and hunger again just as my father fed your fathers with manna in the wilderness and they hungered afterwards. Nevertheless, I have bread to feed you that you will eat and never hunger anymore. Then the people said, give us the bread that we may eat and hunger no more.

³³For the bread of God is he which cometh down from heaven, and giveth life unto the world. ³⁴Then said they unto him, Lord, evermore give us this bread.” John 6:33, 34 (KJV)

Howbeit, Jesus made it plain to the people that He is the bread and anyone who wants to live must first eat His flesh and drink His blood.

“⁵¹I am the living bread which came down from heaven: if any man eat of this bread, he shall live for ever: and the bread that I will give is my flesh, which I will give for the life of the world. ⁵²The Jews

therefore strove among themselves, saying, How can this man give us his flesh to eat? [53]Then Jesus said unto them, Verily, verily, I say unto you, Except ye eat the flesh of the Son of man, and drink his blood, ye have no life in you. [54]Whoso eateth my flesh, and drinketh my blood, hath eternal life; and I will raise him up at the last day. [55]For my flesh is meat indeed, and my blood is drink indeed. [56]He that eateth my flesh, and drinketh my blood, dwelleth in me, and I in him. [57]As the living Father hath sent me, and I live by the Father: so he that eateth me, even he shall live by me. [58]This is that bread which came down from heaven: not as your fathers did eat manna, and are dead: he that eateth of this bread shall live for ever."

John 6:51-58 (KJV)

The teaching of Jesus to eat His flesh and drink His blood created pandemonium among the people and they all left him. All the multitude left, and Jesus was left with only His twelve (12) disciples. This was the place where Jesus started discussion about the Holy Communion. After the people had left, there was a gap before the consumption of the last supper.

The last Super: It was time for the feast of Passover, a Jewish feast for commemorating their deliverance from slavery in Egypt. Jesus knew His end had come, but the disciples did not know. The disciples discussed the Passover celebrations with Jesus, and He instructed them on what to do.

"[17]Now the first day of the feast of unleavened bread the disciples came to Jesus, saying unto him, Where wilt thou that we prepare for thee to eat the passover? [18] And he said, Go into the city to such a man, and say unto him, The Master saith, My time is at hand; I will keep the passover at thy house with my disciples. [19] And the disciples did as Jesus had appointed them; and they made ready the passover. [20]Now when the even was come, he sat down with the twelve" Matthew 26: 17-20 (KJV).

Unlike, the typical passover celebrated with a big ritual meal known as the "Seder" in Hebrew, where family and friends gather together for a feast, Jesus did something different at this passover.

"[19]And he took bread, and gave thanks, and brake it, and gave unto them, saying, This is my body which is given for you: this do in remembrance of me. [20]Likewise also the cup after supper, saying, This cup is the new testament in my blood, which is shed for you" Luke 22:19-20 (KJV)

At this Passover, Jesus while bidding His disciples farewell, shed more light on His teachings about the eating of His flesh and drinking of His blood, which was still an unsolved mystery to the disciples and the multitude that heard it. Jesus used this opportunity to solve the mystery by using unleavened bread and wine as symbols of his flesh and blood and commanded the disciples to continue to observe this meal in remembrance of Him.

Revelation to Paul: Paul was not originally part of the twelve Apostles. After his conversion, God called him to become an Apostle to the Gentiles. Accordingly, he received manifold revelations from God including the revelations of the Holy Communion.

> [23]For I have received of the Lord that which also I delivered unto you, That the Lord Jesus the same night in which he was betrayed took bread: [24]And when he had given thanks, he brake it, and said, Take, eat: this is my body, which is broken for you: this do in remembrance of me. [25]After the same manner also he took the cup, when he had supped, saying, This cup is the new testament in my blood:

this do ye, as oft as ye drink it, in remembrance of me. ²⁶For as often as ye eat this bread, and drink this cup, ye do shew the Lord's death till he come"
-I Corinthians 11:23-26 (KJV)

The revelation of the Holy Communion to Paul added that as often as we conduct the Holy Communion, we commemorate the death of Jesus till His second coming.

In the Revelation of the symbolic, the benefits of the Holy Communion abounds:

(1)   The more often you partake of the Holy Communion, the more you remember Jesus Christ's death, ascension and second coming. Hence, it is advisable to partake of the Holy Communion as often as you can to prepare you for His coming. Some churches do it every day, I do it at home often

(2)   Eating the flesh of Jesus Christ, by the revelation I received, is akin to transplanting the flesh of Jesus into the partaker's flesh. Therefore, on exchanging the partaker's flesh with the flesh of Jesus Christ, this transplant will transform the partaker's flesh into the supernatural the flesh of Jesus Christ

(3)   The drinking of the wine — the blood of Jesus, is like a blood transfusion that cleanses or

replaces the partaker's blood with the blood of Jesus Christ. Most human diseases are connected to the blood. Therefore, the Holy Communion brings healing to all manners of sicknesses.

(4)		The more often you partake of the Holy Communion the more you should stay away from sin. [27]Wherefore whosoever shall eat this bread, and drink this cup of the Lord, unworthily, shall be guilty of the body and blood of the Lord. [28]But let a man examine himself, and so let him eat of that bread, and drink of that cup"

I Corinthians 11:27, 28 (KJV).

It is highly recommended that no one partake of the Holy Communion unworthily. Therefore, let everyone examine themselves and repent of every sin before partaking of the Holy Communion.

Cross

Etsy: Jesus on the cross, wall crosses, Renaissance jesus. Pinterest. (2020, July 16). Retrieved February 18, 2023, from https://www.pinterest.ca/pin/347692033735172822/

Jesus Christ was neither the first nor the last person to be crucified (death on the cross). But Jesus' crucifixion is not comparable to any other; it has spiritual implications. In time past, death by the cross was the most brutal punishment that could be meted upon a victim who was condemned to death.

During the crucifixion of Jesus, Israel was under the rule of the Romans. The Roman's crucifixion process was very cruel and entailed shaming, stripping naked, scourging, carrying of own-cross outside the city, being nailed to the cross, hanging on the cross and finally breaking of the bones of the victim to fast-track their death.

Contemporary religious scholars believed that the Rome tended not to crucify its own citizens because death by crucifixion was an extremely shameful way to die. Instead, thieves, slaves, disgraced soldiers, Christians, foreigners, people accursed or considered treacherous were subjected to crucifixion. Nevertheless, the Romans practiced crucifixion for over 500 years, until Constantine the first abolished it in the fourth century A.D.

In Jesus' days, candidates for crucifixion were people of vile character, those accursed, thieves, slaves, disgraced soldiers and treacherous people convicted of felony. Jesus had none of the characteristics of these people, why was He then crucified? Superficially speaking, it was a case of miscarriage of justice, the Jews accused Him of calling Himself the son of God or King, falsely accusing Jesus of instigating rebellion against the Roman government. None of these accusations were substantiated, but Jesus went through death on the cross as a substitute to take the place of the believers in Him.

"13And Pilate, when he had called together the chief priests and the rulers and the people, 14Said unto them, Ye have brought this man unto me, as one that perverteth the people: and, behold, I, having examined him before you, have found no fault in this man touching those things whereof ye accuse him" Luke 23:13, 14 (KJV)

Prophet Isaiah foretold it: Prophet Isaiah predicted the virgin birth of Jesus and the nature of his death characterized by features associated with crucifixion.

"3He is despised and rejected of men; a man of sorrows, and acquainted with grief: and we hid as it were our faces from him; he was despised, and we esteemed him not. 4Surely he hath borne our griefs, and carried our sorrows: yet we did esteem him stricken, smitten of God, and afflicted. 5But he was wounded for our transgressions, he was bruised for our iniquities: the chastisement of our peace was upon him; and with his stripes we are healed" Isaiah 53: 3-5 (KJV)

Jesus, the second person in the triune God was born as a baby boy and went through normal growth like an average human, but He was God and did not commit any sin. He was a rabbi and well respected leader with followers. But it was prophesied that He would be sorrowful, despised and rejected by men, afflicted and bear the iniquities of everyone, and He would be chastised and beaten for our peace and healing. These happened during Jesus trials and crucifixion. Therefore, the crucifixion of Jesus was a milestone in the healing and salvation of mankind.

Jesus foretold it: During Jesus' ministry on earth, he foretold the similitude of his crucifixion and sometimes the circumstances that would surround his death.

"14And as Moses lifted up the serpent in the wilderness, even so must the Son of man be lifted up: 15That whosoever believeth in him should not perish, but have eternal life"
- John 3:14, 15 (KJV)

When a Pharisee and ruler of the Jews named Nicodemus came to Jesus by night to make enquiries about the miracles He was doing, Jesus explained to him deep divine truths that were difficult for him to comprehend. First, Jesus told Nicodemus the necessity to be born again in order to see the kingdom of God. Secondly, He told Nicodemus about the requirement to be born of water and of the Spirit before anyone can enter the kingdom of God. Thirdly, Jesus told Nicodemus that as Moses lifted the serpent in the wilderness, so shall He (Jesus) be lifted (on the cross) in the world.

Similitude of the Serpent lifted: Israel sinned against God in the wilderness during their exodus to the promise land. The anger of God was upon them and snakes invaded the camps of the Israelites. The snakes were biting the people of Israel and they were dying in their thousands per day. Fortunately, the people repented and cried out to Moses to beseech God on their behalf for His forgiveness and mercy. Moses hearkened to the cry of the people, prayed to God and God answered Moses, instructing him to make a bronze snake and hang it on a tree at the centre of the camp.

"⁷Therefore the people came to Moses, and said, We have sinned, for we have spoken against the LORD, and against thee; pray unto the LORD, that he take away the serpents from us. And Moses prayed for the people. [8]And the LORD said unto Moses, Make thee a fiery serpent, and set it upon a pole: and it shall come to pass, that every one that is bitten, when he looketh upon it, shall live. [9]And Moses made a serpent of brass, and put it upon a pole, and it came to pass, that if a serpent had bitten any man, when he beheld the serpent of brass, he lived" Numbers 21: 7-9 (KJV)

Revelation of the symbolic: Numbers 21: 8, 9 cannot be clearer than the revelation of Jesus Christ in John 3:14, 15. As Moses lifted the bronze serpent in the wilderness so shall Jesus be lifted in the world. As everyone that looked up by faith to the bronze snake on the pole was healed, so shall everyone that looks up by faith to Jesus on the cross be healed and have eternal life.

I am not promoting the worship of the cross here, but the benefits of looking up to Jesus on the cross. I am a Pentecostal Christian, who does not fancy "worshipping" the cross, I am only sharing with you exactly what I received in the revelation I had. It is left for every individual to act according to their convictions. Personally, after receiving this revelation of the symbolism of Jesus on the cross, I bought a cross that is hanging on one of the walls in my house.

Furthermore, the nailing of Jesus on the cross, His victorious statement "it is finished', his burial, descent into hell to take keys of death and hell, and his resurrection all marked the successful accomplishment of the salvation plan of God for mankind, and of course the consummation of everything at His second coming.

Passover

S. S., By, -, Stefan SilverStefan Silver serves as a pastor at Kerem-El (God's Vineyard), Silver, S., & Stefan Silver serves as a pastor at Kerem-El (God's Vineyard). (2021, April 12). What does "passover" really mean? " Kehila News Israel. Kehila News Israel. Retrieved February 18, 2023, from https://news.kehila.org/what-does-passover-really-mean/

As I was writing this book, the world experienced the outbreak of the COVID-19 Pandemic in the early part of the year 2020. The revelation of the Passover in relation to the blood of Jesus Christ was given to me. Since then, I have activated the covenant of the Passover in the blood of Jesus by faith as often as possible. I recommend this same practise to you as long as your level of faith permits it.

"[1]Now the Lord spoke to Moses and Aaron in the land of Egypt, saying, [2]"This month shall be your beginning of months; it shall be the first month of the year to you. [3]Speak to all the congregation of Israel, saying: 'On the tenth of this month every man shall take for himself a lamb, according to the house of his father, a lamb for a household. [4]And if the household is too small for the lamb, let him and his neighbor next to his house take it according to the number of the persons; according to each man's need you shall make your count for the lamb. [5]Your lamb shall be without[a] blemish, a male [b]of the first year. You may take it from the sheep or from the goats. [6]Now you shall keep it until the fourteenth day of the same month. Then the whole assembly of the congregation of Israel shall kill it at twilight. [7]And they shall take some of the blood and put it on the two doorposts and on the lintel of the houses where they eat it. [8]Then they shall eat the flesh on that night; roasted in fire, with unleavened bread and with bitter herbs they shall eat it. [9]Do not eat it raw, nor boiled at all with water, but roasted in fire—its head with its legs and its entrails. [10]You shall let none of it remain until morning, and what remains of it until morning you shall burn with fire.

[11]And thus you shall eat it: with a belt on your

waist, your sandals on your feet, and your staff in your hand. So you shall eat it in haste. It is the Lord's Passover. [12]'For I will pass through the land of Egypt on that night, and will strike all the firstborn in the land of Egypt, both man and beast; and against all the gods of Egypt I will execute judgment: I am the Lord. [13]Now the blood shall be a sign for you on the houses where you are. And when I see the blood, I will pass over you; and the plague shall not be on you to destroy you when I strike the land of Egypt" Exodus 12:1-13.

God instructed the people of Israel in Egypt to kill a lamb by households, eat the meat and mark the lintel of the doors of their house with the blood of the lamb. By night, the angel of death passed through the city and killed the first born of every living thing including those of human beings and livestock. But the angel of death passed over every house with the blood of the lamb on the lintel. That was the revelation! Then by faith, I called my family together, invoked the covenant of the Passover in the blood of Jesus Christ, and marked each one's forehead, and the lintel of our doors with the blood of Jesus Christ. I have prayed "This Passover" revelation occasionally in our church and I continue to confess it as often as possible as we pass through the Covid -19 pandemic.

The efficacy of the blood of Jesus Christ trumps in all respect that of the blood of a lamb. Some years ago in a revelation, I was besieged by a battalion of foot soldiers fully armed with guns. They lined up shoulder to shoulder on both sides of a narrow path of up to 500 metres in length that I was supposed to walk through to freedom. But an Angel of God was with me and I said, "I plead the blood of Jesus upon my way" before setting out. As I set out, I began to walk through the midst of the battalion. None shook, attacked or spoke to me. Then, I asked the Angel, can't they talk, move or attack? The angel said to me "they are incapacitated by the blood of Jesus." When, I looked closely, they were all glued to the ground and to each other by the blood of Jesus Christ. That was how I walked through the path to freedom.

God has made provisions to aid Christians in their earthly journey, every believer needs to seek to discover and use them. The Lord says He will never leave us nor forsake us.

"Be strong and of a good courage, fear not, nor be afraid of them: for the Lord thy God, he it is that doth go with thee; he will not fail thee, nor forsake thee"
- Deuteronomy 31:6 (KJV)